LEADERSHIP
FOR
EINSTEINS

How Smart Leaders Bring Out
The Genius In People

DR. JIM SELLNER, PHD., DIPC.

ISBN: 1501007483
ISBN 13: 9781501007484
Library of Congress Control Number: 2014915733
Vancouver, British Columbia

CONTENTS

WHAT IS THIS BOOK?

This book is the culmination of my forty years of learning, practicing, and playing the leadership game - both live and virtually - on the topics of emotional intelligence, management, interpersonal communication, and organizational change.

In addition to cofounding a small business, developing it from nothing into a $1.2 million enterprise, I have coached about four hundred executives over the last sixteen years in Canada, the United States, Brazil, Russia, Iraq, Indonesia, and Denmark.

Through thousands of hours of coaching sessions, I have had the privilege of working with people willing to "pull back the kimono" to explore crucial questions in their roles of leader or manager: What's working well? What do I need to improve? What do I want more of? What do I want less of?

Work relationships are fraught with hopes, dreams, problems, chaos, victories, and disappointments; these elements are natural in any human endeavor.

That's not the problem.

The problem is learning how to develop and apply the skills needed to deal more productively with such turbulence.

Take the following steps to become more effective:

1. Become aware of how your behaviours affect others
2. Change your behaviours to help employees improve
3. Prepare for back-at-work "change-back" reactions
4. Infuse your set of new behaviours with healthier, more productive career-enhancing approaches.

The role of leaders and managers is paradoxical. The outcomes we produce are not solely dependent on the participation of anyone else. In addition, there are no leaders without followers.

Developing skills to better deal with "your own stuff" helps you learn how to deal with difficult situations with coworkers, bosses, or customers.

If you are reading this book, you are likely someone in a leadership or management position. The information provided here will help you to further your own development so you can more easily bring out the genius in others.

My clients - particularly CEOs - often ask, "Why don't people do what they are supposed to do?"

The answer: Because you are a lousy leader!

The challenge is this: Are you willing to do the work to become a great leader?

WHO AM I?

With any piece of how-to content, it's important to know who the author is and what makes him an authority on that particular topic.

So who am I?

My name is Jim Sellner. Regarding education, I have a master's degree in city planning, another master's in humanistic psychology and Eastern philosophies, a doctorate in psychology, and a diploma in individual and group coaching, which included twelve hundred hours of brutally honest feedback from my mentors about my blind spots.

My mentors were not interested in teaching me techniques, although I did learn some good ones. Their philosophy was that using techniques without a highly developed emotional intelligence was manipulative. So they focused on developing my self-awareness, self-management, empathy, social skills, and assertiveness—essentially, my emotional intelligence.

I've also had a string of careers. I've been a city planner, a faculty member at a major university, and a relationship counselor, counseling about one thousand couples.

I have facilitated retreats for the Entrepreneurs Organization (EO), the Young Presidents Organization (YPO), and CAFÉ (the Canadian Association of Family Enterprise).

I also managed a business with thirty employees and cofounded a business that organized forums for CEOs looking to grow personally and professionally. In the ten years I was involved in CEO forums, I worked with about one hundred executives on a monthly basis.

To me, life is a learning experience. Risk nothing. Get nothing.

LEADERSHIP FOR EINSTEINS: HOW SMART LEADERS BRING OUT THE GENIUS IN PEOPLE

Being a leader or manager would be so easy if people just did what they were supposed to do! My coaching clients often ask, "Why don't employees do what they are asked to do?"

Here are some of the reasons.

On the employee's end:

- he or she may not know how to do the task, may not have the competence to complete the task, or may not be motivated to do it.
- a lack of motivation can arise when the employee does not see the value in completing the task or experiences no rewards for good work.
- the employee may think that the manager's way of doing the task will not work or that his or her way is better.
- personal issues or other priorities may be the reason the employee is not doing what he or she is supposed to be doing.

Organizational reasons for poor performance include:

- no rewards for excellent performance;
- no consequences for poor performance;
- poor training of leaders, managers, or supervisors; or other obstacles that prevent the employee from completing the task.

So, the question is this: If you, as the manager, don't deal with poor performance, who is ultimately responsible for the poor performance? If you, as leader or manager, do not develop people into higher performance, how do you think you can be successful?

The answer is that *you* are responsible for people's performance.

Poor performance occurs because of poor leadership, poor management, or both. High performance is a result of a leader or manager engaging with his or her followers to produce desired results.

When managers have the skills to change poor performance into high performance, the result is that jobs are done well. Employees become geniuses. The company is more profitable. People have careers, not just jobs.

Leadership for Einsteins is a system to improve performance so you are more profitable, you save money, you save time and you increase engagement - should you choose to take the assignment.

EINSTEIN - JUST A GUY WHO WAS A GENIUS

In 1999 Einstein was named *Time* magazine's Person of the Century. A poll of prominent physicists named him the greatest physicist of all time. In popular culture his name has become synonymous with genius. At one point in his life, however, Einstein was a lowly technical assistant in the Swiss patent office.

Employees are not dummies or idiots who need to be told what to do. But everyone - like Einstein - could use some guidance to help them discover their internal genius.

Consider the paper clip. If we could convert the mass of a paper clip (0.03 ounces) entirely to energy, how big a punch would it pack?

Einstein's most famous equation, $E = mc^2$, indicates that the energy released would be equivalent to the mass times the speed of light squared. The speed of light is immense - 670 million miles per hour - making the speed of light squared almost inconceivable. So if we could harness the paper clip's power, it would yield the equivalent of eighteen kilotons of TNT. That's roughly the size of the bomb that destroyed Hiroshima in 1945.

Now consider the person. There are about 125 million employees in North America, with a payroll of $4.6 trillion. Research informs us that most employees realize between 20 and 60 percent of their potential performance. Like the paper clip, those 125 million employees represent a massive amount of pent-up energy.

If we, as business leaders, would make the time and effort and provide the resources to help people discover their genius within and how to apply it, the time and impact on people's personal lives and corporations' performance would be immense.

Leadership for Einsteins is a powerful tool that can mobilize people's hearts and minds to channel their energies, abilities, and knowledge. It has a deep, rich foundation of research in biology and psychology as well as practical business applications from thousands of companies worldwide. It has grown out of my work with thousands of leaders over forty years.

$P = MC^3$

Performance is a function of motivation X competence X congratulations X cash

$P = MC^3$ is a process for increasing the five key areas that define a sustainable business: (1) financial intelligence, (2) emotional intelligence, (3) values, vision, and mission, (4) leadership and followership, and (5) commitment to action.

The formula is designed to increase a company's "invisible balance sheet" (Svelby). This involves improving the following factors:

- The reputation of the company
- The number of people who are competent, aligned, and engaged and thus stay longer
- Employees who continually add value to the company
- The number of volunteers minus the number of volun*tolds* in the business

In a company with a healthy invisible balance sheet, people say, *"This is a great place to work. I am proud of this company. I look forward to coming to work. I really enjoy my days off because I can joyfully share the rewards of my work with my family and friends."*

Einstein would work for such a company.

The sign above his door would read:

"We can't solve problems by using the same kind of thinking we used when we created them."

Leadership for Einsteins **is founded in the wisdom as expressed by the quotations below.**

What Got You Here, Will Not Get You There.

Marshall Goldsmith, Executive Coach

The front line produces the bottom line!

Stephen Covey, *The 8th Habit*

We do not make money with happy people. We make money when people are competent and turned on!

David Maister, *First Among Equals*

Prescription without diagnosis is management malpractice.

Neville Joffe, President, Financial Accountability Means Everyone

There has to be a change of thinking between thinking like a manager/ owner and...creating business people who think and act like owners. People need to know the rules, how to keep score, and how to win.

Jack Stack, *The Great Game of Business*

As goes the leadership team, so goes the rest of the firm. Whatever strengths or weaknesses exist within the organization can be traced right back to the cohesion of the business owner and/or executive team and their levels of risk management, competencies, discipline, respect, and alignment to the vision/mission.

Verne Harnish, *Mastering the Rockefeller Habits*

Conditions change. People change. But the scientific laws of human behavior are constant. They always are working for your business.

Aubrey Daniels, known as the father of performance management

PROFITABILITY, LEADERSHIP, AND THE INVISIBLE BALANCE SHEET

John Eggers, author of *Profitability, Leadership & the "Invisible Balance Sheet,"* researched three hundred leading entrepreneurial companies worldwide, including many members of the Ernst & Young Entrepreneur of the Year Institute, Profit 100, and Inc. 500.

His research was acknowledged by the American Society for Training and Development as "the first to link leadership to successful entrepreneurship."

In his groundbreaking study of companies that showed long-term profitability and were identified as "employers of choice" (the "Invisible Balance Sheet"), he found that a critical element in a CEO's success is the competence and motivation "to transform employees from people who simply work together, to people who work as part of a highly motivated team, creating and inspiring the willingness to risk...and loyalty in each team member through praise, plus regular corrective feedback... and support of their efforts through formal programs that reward team effort."

Those are great business concepts.

Leadership for Einsteins is designed to help put those ideas into action by showing leaders, managers, and followers how to negotiate a partnership to produce the highest level of competence, alignment, engagement, and performance.

By applying $P = MC^3$, you can create a company of people who take pride of ownership in the organization's overall performance by making the best decisions for both their own benefit and the company's sustainability.

It's about enacting the genius of intelligent self-interest.

SO WHO ARE THESE GENIUSES?

Geniuses in the workplace are smart people who can make enormous contributions. At the same time, they can be a manager's worst nightmare, as they can be obnoxious, arrogant, rebellious, and antisocial, with no regard for corporate protocol. Yet most managers would shrivel up in a corner if the genius left for a better job.

Geniuses are people who thrive on solving problems. They want to be congratulated for their accomplishments. This doesn't mean that they strive for rapid ascent up the corporate ladder; they just want to be respected, receive fair pay, and enjoy doing their job.

CHARACTERISTICS OF GENIUSES

Geniuses are intelligent in terms of logic, spatial relationships, systems, mathematics, and problem solving. They are also emotionally intelligent—self-aware, able to manage their emotions, and respectful of others. In addition to being team players, they have an excellent work ethic. They work until the problem is solved, the product is shipped, or the service is completed.

Geniuses relish a challenge, frequently working nonstop until a problem is solved. They are naturally curious about things and people, and so they thrive on experimenting, tinkering, fixing, and adapting. Geniuses are fascinated by the intricacies and complex workings of the world. While they can be either introverts or extroverts, they lean towards introversion. However, they do enjoy exchanging ideas with other geniuses. Lastly, they are reflective thinkers: they think before speaking and mull over problems.

In short, geniuses are smart, mobile, and dedicated more to their craft than to status. Genius resides in every woman and every man.

From my own experience, they're the type of colleague I don't want to talk to unless (a) I know what I'm talking about, (b) I don't know what I'm talking about and admit it, or (c) I want to find out what I don't know.

You should refrain from faking or trying to impress a genius. You will be viewed a fake, a fool, and a phony. You will lose credibility, which could be difficult to recoup unless you admit to (b), which a genius will readily forgive.

So the question is this: dummies, idiots, or geniuses - which do you prefer to develop on your team?

LEADERSHIP FOR EINSTEINS: P = MC³ INSIGHTS

$$P = MC^3$$

Intuition

Nowledge

Self-Awareness

Inspiration

Genius

History/Herstory

Time

Senses

DUMMIES, IDIOTS, OR GENIUSES - WHICH DO YOU PREFER?

The genius of any leadership theory is based on measures of financial outcomes so it is considered to be successful, relevant, and applicable.

A practical leadership intervention will link the leader or manager, financial impacts, and company outcomes with standard company financial metrics.

The theory must link directly with valuation outcomes for the company. This link is the only way an intervention will be relevant to a company whose aim is the creation and enhancement of shareholder value.

Every business leader's job is to help employees acquire the competencies, knowledge, and motivation needed to fully use their unique talents that will help to increase the company's financial performance, at the same time building its "invisible balance sheet."

A leader's style will effect followers' competencies and motivation and will either promote or inhibit both human and financial performance.

$P = MC^3$

Performance is a function of motivation X competence X congratulations X cash.

Motivation is the willingness to keep going in spite of setbacks.

Competence is the ability to carry out a specific task or goal to *consistently* produce the desired results.

Congratulations means acknowledging when a job has been done well, when the employee has shown progress, or when the person has given it his or her best shot.

Cash refers to paying people fairly for their consistent, demonstrated levels of competence, experience, and engagement.

*"If you praise people but don't raise them, they can't pay their bills.
If you raise their pay, but don't praise them, it won't cure their ills."*
John C. Maxwell, The 3600 Leader

AN OUTRAGEOUS PROPOSAL

For every employee that you pay $50,000 annually, not counting benefits, go to the bank and take out $5,000 of your hard-earned cash.

If you have five employees, that's $25,000 per year. If you have ten employees, that's $50,000. If your company has one hundred employees, that amounts to $500,000 annually, and if you have two hundred employees, that's $1 million.

Now, take that money and burn it.

That's right, burn it!

You're thinking, *"This is nuts. Are you crazy? Why would I do that?"* Well, that's what you are doing right now, every day, month, and year. You are throwing your hard-earned cash into the garbage.

How? Why?

Because that's what absenteeism, turnover, disability costs, workplace accidents, workers' compensation, lawsuits, poorly developed competencies, poorly made products, waste, and low engagement cost you.

The truth is, every person in your company—except for you, of course—is at least 10 percent less effective than he or she could be. Many of your employees are performing at 20 percent, 30 percent, 40 percent, or even 50 percent of their potential.

Ka-ching$

The sad fact is they don't like being that way no matter what you may think!

NOW FOR BRUTAL FACT NUMBER TWO!

If your employees are not performing up to their potential, then you, as a leader or manager, are not, either. You are even less effective than your most ineffective employee.

Why?

Because you are not leveraging people's genius - their unique talents. You might even be rewarding them for acting like dummies or idiots.

In effect, you are saying to your employees, "It's OK to waste your time and efforts. As a matter of fact, no matter how much time and effort you waste, I'll pay you even more each year! And, on top of that, I will hire more people to do what you could be doing with less effort and more pride."

Sound crazy? It is! But that's what's going on in your company, and almost every company in the world.

DON'T BELIEVE IT?

A ten-year study published in the *Harvard Business Review* showed that employees and managers spend about 50 percent to 90 percent of their time in unproductive busywork.

A mere 10 percent of managers spend their time in a committed, successful, and reflective manner with the intent of increasing productivity.

Wow! Ten percent!

Harris Interactive, originators of the Harris Poll, recently polled twenty-three thousand American residents employed full-time within key industries and in key functional areas.[1]

The poll's most stunning findings:

- Only 37 percent of employees said they have a clear understanding of what their organization is trying to achieve, and why— 63 percent said, *"Huh?"*
- Only 20 percent were enthusiastic about their team's and company's goals. That means 80 percent were not!
- Only 15 percent felt that their organization fully enables them to execute key goals. Wow - 85 percent can't execute properly!
- Only 10 percent believe their company holds people accountable. I guess employees are sleeping!

And the worst part of it is that it's not just about the money.

It's about people's spirit, their sense of self-respect, and the satisfaction of being part of a company that values, rewards, recognizes, and assists people to experience a blend of joy and abundance.

It's about creating a profitable company that's also a great place to work.

Ka-ching$$

In 2006, 43 percent of US workers called in sick when they actually felt fine. That's up from 35 percent in 2005.[2] That's a lot of wasted money and human spirit.

DISABILITY EQUALS MONEY

In a survey conducted by Watson Wyatt Worldwide, 56 percent of respondents claimed employees are suffering from more stress, depression, and other mental-health issues. Long-term disability claims rose 27 percent since 2003.[3]

THE LEADERSHIP VACUUM

In 2002 Watson Wyatt Worldwide conducted a study of 12,750 workers in the United States to determine how aligned they were to organizational goals.

Only 9 percent of the respondents - one in ten employees - had a very high level of commitment to organizational goals.

The picture becomes more dismal: 34 percent reported they are only somewhat, barely, or not at all engaged.

To top it off, only 58 percent of workers surveyed believe that their employers even have goals.[4]

Ka-ching$$

GET THE $5,000 BACK WITH P = MC³

- Reduce absenteeism. Effective leadership creates engaged employees who don't book off as much. Time lost for personal reasons increased from 7.4 days per worker in 1977 to 9.8 days in 2005 (Statistics Canada). At $180 per day for 9.8 days, that comes to $1,764 per employee, which does not include the time used to plan those days off.

- Decrease turnover costs. People are less likely to leave great leadership or competent managers. Cost of replacement is generally at least one year's salary, plus the indirect expenses from the learning curve, organizational intelligence, morale, internal and customer relationships.

- Cut disability. Costs go down when leaders and managers are effective. The Canadian Mental Health Association estimates that stress costs Canadian businesses $5 billion annually.

- Avoid workplace accidents. Well-managed employees have fewer accidents.[5]

- Shrink workers' compensation. Claims and lawsuits decrease when a company is committed to developing its employees.[6]

- Build the competency-motivation interaction. Increased competencies means people are more inspired to perform better. Highly motivated, engaged people look for ways to do things better, which translates into higher profits per employee.

For a free tool to figure out the impact of $P = MC^3$ on performance, go to www.subject2change.ca/LfE/ROI

LEADERSHIP FOR EINSTEINS: P = MC³

WHICH WOULD YOU PREFER?

Would you rather increase revenue per employee or profit per employee? One high-performance employee equals three good ones.

The Container Store, a privately held retailer out of Texas named one of the top places to work in the United States the past five years, has a simple productivity formula: one great employee replaces three good; pay them twice as much ($18 per hour vs. the standard $9 a typical retailer pays) while having a lower total wage cost; and provide each employee with 160 hours of training.

In essence, fewer higher-paid, smart people are preferable to many low-paid "dummies."

It's your choice.

And if you're having a tough time recruiting employees, consider that the Container Store had 4,000 people apply for the 40 positions when they opened their latest retail store in New York City.

Kip Tindell and Garrett Boone, the cofounders, are choosing to lead![7]

- Pay that one well-led, well-trained performer twice as much.
- The outcome will be lower total wages and higher profits.

How do you do this? You must increase profit per employee by developing people's competencies and giving out congratulations and cash.

QUESTION TO SELF

"Would I rather have sixty low-paid, unmotivated, poor performers, or twenty, well-paid high performers?"

Verne Harnish, *The Growth Guy*

MISSION POSSIBLE

Now imagine that each of your employees goes to the bank, takes out $5,000, and then willingly, happily, gives it back to the company.

Remember, that's only a 10 percent improvement in performance.

A well-designed leadership development program will increase performance by 30 to 60 percent, or $15,000 to $30,000 per employee.

That money goes right to the bottom line.

Equally important, the company will have a healthier "invisible balance sheet" because people will be more competent, aligned, and engaged.

Don't think so? Think again.

The Gap and LensCrafters have done just that. The Gap, Baby Gap, Old Navy, and Banana Republic invested in a performance-based leadership program.

The results of the program:

- On $1 billion in revenue, the companies saved almost $2 million and generated $14 million.
- Employees increased conversion rates in the first nine months of 2003 by two points. If annualized, this increase would generate an additional $8.4 million in revenue.
- They achieved a 10 percent decrease in shrink.
- Turnover decreased by 10 percent.
- Overall store manager turnover decreased from 14.4 percent in 2002 to 3.7 percent in 2003.
- Cost per employee for the training about $6,000.
- ROI cost saving per participant was about $8,000.

- ROI with increased revenues totaled about $64,000 per employee.[8]

Need more proof? Consider the outcomes LensCrafters saw just six months after introducing a performance-based leadership intervention:

- Managers were significantly more effective on a day-to-day basis. That translated into total and comparative store sales increasing to record levels.
- Seven of nine customer-satisfaction scales showed statistically significant increases.

Company earnings continued to rise in the year following the intervention. In addition, turnover decreased 7.7 percent, which decreased hiring and training costs.[9]

To check out how productive, in dollars, your team is, go to www.vivoteam.com

RESEARCH FROM ACCENTURE

Once the right talent has been identified and recruited, how do you equip them with the critical knowledge needed to be high performers?

Consider the second key talent management lever—learning.

Research shows that companies with high-performance learning organizations returned better revenue and profit growth compared to their competitors and industry peers:

- Productivity (as measured by sales per employee) was 27 percent greater.
- Revenue growth was 40 percent higher.
- Net income growth was 50 percent greater.
- For every $1.00 invested in training, the ROI was $2.43."[10,11]

Leader Self-Awareness: The First Step to Emotional Intelligence

Leadership is the ability and willingness to influence others and be influenced by them in order to develop people's genius while delivering business results.

Self-awareness is having an accurate picture of your strengths and limitations, the willingness to seek out and act on feedback, the willingness to admit mistakes, and the ability to reflect on how your actions impact others.

Leadership and management are different and complementary.

- Leadership is about getting things right, like strategy, values, vision, and mission.
- Management is teaching ordinary people how to do the right things exceptionally well, consistently, and on time.

The methods in *Leadership for Einsteins* apply to both leaders and managers.

To start elevating your emotional intelligence, complete the self-assessment provided in the following pages to get some insights into your leadership and management styles.

Why? Because the first small step to improving your competence is becoming aware of your impact on others.

We can't solve problems by using the same kind of thinking we used when we created them.

—Albert Einstein

Key operating principles of *Leadership for Einsteins:*

- Leadership and management must go hand in hand.
- Workers need their managers not only to assign tasks but also to define purpose.
- Managers must organize workers to maximize efficiency while also nurturing skills, developing talent, and inspiring results.

LEADERS' ACHILLES' HEEL - LACK OF SELF-AWARENESS

The Dunning-Kruger effect is the phenomenon wherein people who have little knowledge tend to think that they know more than they do, while others who have much more knowledge tend to think that they know less than they actually do. Dunning and Kruger were awarded a 2000 Nobel Prize for their work.[12]

The phenomenon was demonstrated in a series of experiments at Cornell University. Their results were published in the *Journal of Personality and Social Psychology* in December of 1999.

Dunning-Kruger noted that in many skill areas, "ignorance more frequently begets confidence than does knowledge."

They hypothesized that with a typical skill, people may possess to a greater or lesser degree, the following:

- Incompetent individuals tend to overestimate their own level of skill.
- Incompetent individuals fail to recognize genuine skill in others.
- Incompetent individuals fail to recognize the degree of their inadequacy.
- If they can be trained to substantially improve their own skill level, these people can recognize and acknowledge their own previous lack of skill.

In a series of studies, Kruger and Dunning examined self-assessments of logical reasoning skills, grammatical skills, and humor. After being shown their test scores, the subjects were again asked to estimate their own rank.

The competent group members accurately estimated their rank while the incompetent group members still overestimated their own rank.

As Dunning and Kruger noted, "People with true knowledge tended to underestimate their (skill-specific) competence.

A follow-up study suggests that grossly incompetent students improve both their skill level and their ability to estimate their class rank only after extensive, intensive tutoring in the skills they had previously lacked."[13]

The implications for leaders and managers are far-reaching. If you are incompetent in leadership or management skills there is no way you can help your followers because you are blind to what people need.

SELF-ASSESSMENT OF YOUR LEADER STYLE

Using the assessment below, you can begin to increase your leadership strengths and identify areas for improvement. This will help you to better work with people so they're more able and inclined to do what they should be doing.

The assessment will help you to take actions in your daily work to improve your leadership and management skills.

Please assess yourself honestly.

If you truly want to develop the leader within, complete the assessment, read the rest of the book, and then work on Step 6 - Negotiate for Performance. It's worth your efforts.

SELF-ASSESSMENT

The following twenty-five statements will help you assess your leader style. As you read each statement, think of a typical situation.

Please use the following scale:

1. Hardly ever
2. Not very often
3. Sometimes
4. Most of the time
5. Always

Please circle the number that applies to each statement.

1. I check my employees' work on a regular basis to assess their progress and learning. 1 2 3 4 5

2. I hold periodic meetings to clarify company policy and mission and to ask for feedback. 1 2 3 4 5

3. I assign people into task groups to deal with policies that affect them. 1 2 3 4 5

4. I provide my direct reports with clear responsibilities and allow them to decide how to accomplish them. 1 2 3 4 5

5. I make sure people are aware of and understand all company policies and procedures. 1 2 3 4 5

6. I recognize individual achievements with encouragement and by giving feedback on behaviours that need correcting. 1 2 3 4 5

7. I discuss any organizational or policy changes with my team before taking action. 1 2 3 4 5

8. I discuss the organization's strategic mission with my team 1 2 3 4 5

9. I show people who are learning new tasks the how's and why's of doing those new tasks. 1 2 3 4 5

10. I meet with my team regularly to discuss what's working well and what needs improving. 1 2 3 4 5

11. I avoid making judgments of people's ideas or suggestions and, when appropriate, provide feedback about their ideas. 1 2 3 4 5

12. I ask my direct reports to think ahead and develop long-term plans for their jobs 1 2 3 4 5

13. I set down performance standards for each aspect of my employees' jobs.   1 2 3 4 5

14. I explain the benefits of achieving work goals to my team
                                                            1 2 3 4 5

15. I rotate the role of team-meeting leader amongst different people.   1 2 3 4 5

16. I periodically review the importance of quality, and I ask my team to establish the control standards.   1 2 3 4 5

17. I ask that people report back to me after completing each step of their work when they are working on a new task.   1 2 3 4 5

18. I hold regular meetings to discuss work status and to get feedback.   1 2 3 4 5

19. I provide my team with the time and resources to pursue their own developmental objectives after we have clarified them together.   1 2 3 4 5

20. I ask people to create their own goals and objectives and submit them to me in finished form.   1 2 3 4 5

21. I usually assign work in small, easily controlled units. 1 2 3 4 5

22. I focus on opportunities and use problems and mistakes to help people improve.   1 2 3 4 5

23. I wait to evaluate problems and concerns until they are discussed.   1 2 3 4 5

24. I ask for clarification instead of giving solutions.   1 2 3 4 5

25. I make sure that information systems are timely and accurate and that information is fed directly to the right people.   1 2 3 4 5

LEADER STYLE SCORE SHEET

In order to score the self-assessment, please group your responses into four categories in the grid below.

STEP ONE

Look at the grid below. It is divided into four sections.
Each section lists the statement numbers from the questionnaire.

STEP TWO

For each statement number, transfer the number you circled.
For example, if you circled 4 for statement 11, you would put 4 beside statement 11.

STEP THREE

To calculate the total score for each section, add all the individual statement scores for each section.

YOUR PREFERRED STYLES QUADRANT

FOCUSING · *Hi Showing, Hi Encouraging*		**FACILITATING** · *Lo Showing, Hi Encouraging*	
2 _____		3 _____	
6 _____		7 _____	
10 _____		11 _____	
14 _____		15 _____	
18 _____		19 _____	
22 _____	**Total** _____	23 _____	**Total** _____
SHOWING · *HI Showing, Lo Encouraging*		**DELEGATING** · *Lo Showing, Lo Encouraging*	
1 _____		4 _____	
5 _____		8 _____	
9 _____		12 _____	
13 _____		16 _____	
17 _____		20 _____	
21 _____	**Total** _____	24 _____	**Total** _____

Interested in detailed feedback on your styles?
Click www.subject2change.ca/LfE/feedback.

To get your free colour pdf of the four leader styles, click on www.subject2change.ca/LfE/colour

In the following pages, you will discover how you can use each style to work with people to improve their performance.

Note: We have full twenty-item and fifty-item assessments for more insightful, accurate insights into one's leadership style.

We also have assessments for 360-feedback. This is *the* most accurate assessment of your leadership style: how others perceive your impact on them.

E-mail jim@subject2change.ca to find out more about the importance of you knowing how others perceive your leader style.

WORKING WITH PEOPLE SO THEY ARE DOING WHAT THEY ARE SUPPOSED TO BE DOING

P = MC³ OPERATING PRINCIPLES

- Competence and motivation are task/goal specific.
- Prescription without diagnosis is management malpractice.
- Use the video test to describe behaviours
- Behaviours produce results.
- Competence = Can Do
- Motivation = Am Doing
- Emotional intelligence is the oxygen of leadership.
- Leadership and followership is a team sport.
- The behaviours that you see people doing are the ones you've taught them to do.
- Leadership is a process, not an event.
- You teach people how to treat you.
- Recognize who packs your parachute.
- Serving melts cynicism.
- A leader's or manager's job is to maximize the billion-dollar computer that's housed between people's ears.

$P = MC^3$ A TOOL TO GETTING PEOPLE TO DO WHAT THEY ARE SUPPOSED TO BE DOING

STEP 1: GET CLEAR ON "THE DEAL" TO SET THE CONTEXT FOR ENGAGEMENT

Get clear on *"The Deal"* - what the company is offering its employees and what the company expects from its employees.

"The Deal" enhances the personal and professional growth of the right people doing the right things in the company and thus promotes engagement.

We want people to be engaged, aligned, competent, and motivated. We want engaged volunteers, not disengaged volun*tolds*.

Getting clear on *"The Deal"* means creating a partnership in which everyone understands the expectations and the benefits of working for the company. This includes **showing** people how to do the job well, **focusing** on improvement, **facilitating** development, and **delegating** to self-reliant achievers.

In negotiating *"The Deal"*, the employer and employee clarify their expectations.

"The Deal" arises out of a two-way conversation that results in a clear agreement. When leaders have clear deals with their team members those team members identify with the company and leader. People feel good about working in the company. They start off on the right foot.

"People are not our most important asset. The right people are our most important asset. First, get the right people on the bus, the wrong people off the bus, and the right people in the right seats - then figure out where to drive the bus." Jim Collins, *Good to Great*

Getting clear on *"The Deal"* tells us, up front, whether we've got the right person on the bus.

Finally, *"The Deal"* fulfills three crucial employee-employer relationships:

1. **Perceived mutual purpose.** This is the entrance condition to employee engagement. Usually it's there, but people don't know it. There must be an agreed-upon purpose that each participant shares. Southwest Airlines and Starbucks spend a lot of time and money developing this perceived mutual purpose in people.

2. **Understood mutual respect.** This is a continuance condition. It says, *"I know you care about and respect me because of the way you treat me."* To build respect in a relationship, leaders and managers must create dialogue with - not lecture to - the person or group.

3. **A mutual commitment to be motivated, competent, engaged, and aligned.** This is a basic condition of good relationships.

It is the mechanism by which progress, or lack thereof, is measured.

Vancity, Canada's largest credit union, designated by *MacLean's* magazine in 2004 as the number-one place to work in Canada for its twenty-five hundred employees, has $17.5 billion in assets, and about five hundred thousand members at forty-seven branches.

Here is how Vancity does *"The Deal."*[14]

"At Vancity we will:

- Provide you with an inspiring vision of how you can make a meaningful difference to your community through the work that you do.
- Offer a diverse and flexible learning environment that challenges you to build on your strengths and gain new ones.
- Take the time to celebrate our successes, and foster a culture that encourages employees to recognize one another in meaningful ways for a job well done.
- Support you in striking a work-life dynamic that's right for you, and generously reward you and your family for your passion, contribution and commitment to Vancity.

While we are committed to being a great place to work, we expect a lot from our employees.

It's a partnership.

So here's what Vancity asks of you:

- Live the Vancity values/take personal responsibility.
- Manage your own career.
- Be authentic.
- Take initiative.
- Support your team.
- Create community.
- Push yourself to think out of the box.
- Have fun."

Get *"The Deal"* clear in the job interview.

Infuse *"The Deal"* into the new hire in the first thirty days to get engagement right off the bat.

Make sure *"The Deal"* is reinforced in the onboarding process.

WHAT IS "THE DEAL" WITH YOUR COMPANY?

The top three things that my company expects from me are:

1. _____
2. _____
3. _____

The three most important things that my company offers me are:

1. _____
2. _____
3. _____

Do these six things motivate me to be engaged with my company?

YES   NO

If your answer was YES, answer the following:

How do I show that?

If your answer was NO, answer the following:
Is there anything I might do to change that?
Is it time to leave?

ACTIVATE "THE DEAL" WITH YOUR BOSS AND TEAM MEMBERS

Sharing this information with your boss would be a useful career development exercise for you. It would help you to get clear on *"The Deal"* with her or him.

Your next career development step would be to ask each of your team to fill out What Is *"The Deal"* with Your Company. Then ask your team members to divide themselves into trios or pairs to discuss their results. Engaging in this process will result in your team getting clear on the deal, increase engagement while improving individual and team performance.

Your job during the above process to help clear up any confusion that people may have regarding *"The Deal."* When employees are confused or do not know what the deal is, their engagement will go down.

STEP 2: CREATE ALIGNMENT WITH THE COMPANY'S VALUES, VISION, AND MISSION

When people in leadership positions begin to serve a vision infused with a larger purpose, their work shifts naturally from producing results to encouraging the growth of people who produce results.
Peter Senge, C. Otto Scharmer, Joseph Jaworski, Betty Sue Flowers
Presence: Human Purpose and the Field of the Future[15]

Alignment is the essence of management. Linking is an action, alignment creates performance. Learn them. Communicate them. Align with them. Live them.

Fred Smith, FedEx CEO

Good people move for culture, not money.
Studies have shown that great people look for three things in their employer
(1) Where are we going?
(2) What is our plan to get there?
(3) How do I factor into that plan?
If we can't paint a compelling picture of our corporate vision and culture while answering those questions, we will not be very successful in luring 'A' Players.

Verne Harnish, www.Gazelles.com

When employees understand the values, vision, mission and goals, companies enjoy a 29 percent greater return than other firms.

Watson-Wyatt Work Study[16]

VALUES: WHAT'S IMPORTANT AROUND HERE

"Values - one of those things that can sound soft and squishy, especially in the context of a company. The reality - I have found - is actually quite the opposite. They form the most solid bedrock of any group or organization and really matter to the individuals."

Tim Cadogan, CEO, OpenX

OPENX VALUES ACCORDING TO TIM CADOGAN

- We are one
  One team. No exceptions. We are a group of strong and diverse individuals unified by a clear common purpose.

- Our customers define us
  We know our business flourishes or dies because of our customers.

- OpenX is mine
  We are all owners of OpenX. We stake our personal and professional reputations on the excellence of our work.

- We are an open book
  We are eager to teach and share what we know with others.

- We evolve fast
  We take risks and confront failure openly. We recognize and repeat success aggressively. We actively seek out and provide constructive criticism. Defensiveness is for weaklings!

Values need to be constantly reinforced.
In defining OpenX's values, here are a few of the lessons I learned:

1. *Just like any other group of people, a company benefits from having clear values to define itself and guide behavior.*
2. *There comes a point in most organizations' growth where tacit assumptions and shared, founding beliefs need to be made more formal and explicit.*
3. *The size threshold at which this is necessary can vary a bit depending how tight the team is. Factors like single or multi-location, breadth of disciplines, homogeneity vs. diversity of team, rate of change are all important to consider. But a good rule of thumb is between 50 - 100 people and in general err on the side of earlier vs. later.*
4. *Being explicit means writing the values down in memorable phrases. We tried to avoid generic words and phrases (like "integrity") and use our own unique voice. This makes the values more relatable and reinforces whatever is unique about the culture.*
5. *The process is vital - involving everyone in the creation and codification of the values is really important. The CEO needs to lead but cannot dictate. The process also never ends. We are*

imperfect and there is always more we can do to make our values more top-of-mind and live by them even more deeply and effectively.

6. *Reinforcement is huge - repeat, reward and recognize. As an example of recognition, our culture team now selects one value for each month and the company votes for one person who best characterizes that value.*

7. *Good, honed values can truly help make decisions. Especially the hardest decisions where numbers and analysis alone can't give you the answer and you have think through more intangible factors.*

8. *Modeling behavior based on the values is crucial - especially by anyone in authority, starting with the CEO and the executive team. If the CEO doesn't lead, the values will not stick.*

9. *Be ready to be BS-tested. On occasion employees should - and will - call you out based on the values. While a bit painful, this is really great because it means the values have really taken hold at the root level and are being used multi-directionally.*

10. *Values are a real and rich source of individual and organizational pride."*

Tim Cadogan, CEO, OpenX

VISION - WHERE WE WANT TO GO, WHAT WE WANT TO BE

Some examples of value statements from each of the company's website:

"Five years from now, Paula's will be rated as a "five star" restaurant in the Greater Toronto area by consistently providing the combination of perfectly prepared food and outstanding service that creates an extraordinary dining experience."

"Five years from now, Computer Services Ltd. will have annual revenues of over one million by consistently providing timely, reasonably priced repair and instructional services."

"Within the next five years, ZZZ Tours will become the premier eco-tour company in _____, increasing revenues to 1 million dollars in 2010 by becoming internationally known for the comfort and excitement of the whale-watching tours it offers."

"Within the next five years, the Women's Centre will have helped create a safer, more harmonious community by helping women acquire the education, skills and resources necessary to build self-sufficient prosperous lives."

"Within the next five years, Metromanage.com will become a leading provider of management software to North American small businesses by providing customizable, user-friendly software scaled to small business needs."

"Five years from now, Tiny Tots Diaper Service will be the top grossing diaper service in the Lower Mainland by consistently providing a reliable, affordable service for Moms and Dads with small children."

MISSION — A STATEMENT ABOUT HOW WE'LL GET THERE

THE CONTAINER STORE

Below is the Container Store's selling philosophy. We use it to illustrate how The Container Store tries to astonish our customers by exceeding their expectations.

"Imagine a man lost in the desert. He's been wandering for weeks. He stumbles across an oasis, where he's offered a glass of water, because surely he must be thirsty. But if you stop to think about what he's experienced and what his needs really are, you know that he needs more than just water. He needs food, a comfortable place to sleep, a phone to call his wife and family, maybe a pair of shoes and a hat to screen the sun's rays.

When a customer comes to our store looking for shoe storage, for example, we equate her to a "Man in a Desert," in desperate need of a complete solution (not just a drink of water). We start asking questions about what her needs are. "How many shoes do you have?" "If shoes are a big problem for you, how does the rest of the closet function?" By anticipating her needs, we know that she needs an organization plan - a complete solution - for her entire closet.

Most retailers are pleased with helping her find a shoe rack - that glass of water - but not at The Container Store. We don't just stop with the obvious. Providing our customers with a complete solution through our Man in the Desert selling philosophy has been key to achieving one of our main goals of having our customers dancing in their organized closet, pantry, home office, etc., because they are so delighted and thrilled with the complete solution we provided them."

But no matter how cleverly you articulate your values, vision, and mission, the absolute number-one thing you must do is repeat and repeat and repeat the message until every employee can voice and deliver on the company's values, vision, and mission. Without that discipline, you're just blowing in the wind.

MY COMPANY'S...

Values _____

Vision _____

Mission _____

QUESTIONS TO SELF

- Do I know - by heart - my company's values, vision, and mission?
  Yes? Recite.
  No? Find out.

- Do I believe my company?
  Yes? Why?
  No? Why not?

- Do those values, vision, and mission inspire me to do good work every day?
  Yes? How does that make me feel?
  No? How does that affect me personally?

HOW TO MAKE SURE EVERYONE UNDERSTANDS THE VALUES, VISION, AND MISSION

Articulate your understanding of the company's values, vision, and mission to your boss. It could be a useful career development move for you.

Your next step would be to ask each of your team to fill out the values, vision, mission statements using the above form. Then ask your team members to divide themselves into trios or pairs to discuss their results. Engaging in this process will result in your team getting clear on the values, vision and mission while increasing engagement and team performance.

Be prepared to help your team members spell out the values, vision and mission. In most companies employees do not have a very good understanding of them.

Step 1: – Get Clear on *"The Deal"*

Step 2: – Align Your People with the Company's Values, Vision, and Mission.

STEP 3: DEFINE THE SPECIFIC TASK OR GOAL

Defining the specific task or goal requires three elements:

- getting clear on the what, how, who, and when
- mobilizing goal efforts
- encouraging task persistence to increase performance

Task or goal clarity does seven things:

- directs attention.
- mobilizes task efforts
- encourages task persistence
- facilitates development of tasks and goals connected to strategy
- makes it possible to measure progress or regression
- makes it possible to identify and correct roadblocks to success
- separates high and low performers

SMARTER tasks or goals are specific, measureable, achievable, recorded, time measured, ethical, and responsible.

THE SPECIFIC TASKS AND GOALS OF A MANAGER

What do managers do?

One answer to this question comes from the late Peter Drucker, whose name stands out above the others in the century-long history of management studies.

Drucker worked as a journalist and studied economics. At some point in his work, he had an epiphany: *"Economists,"* he realized, *"were interested in the behavior of commodities, while [he] was interested in the behavior of people.*"[17]

That led him to, in effect, create the modern study of management.

Drucker divided the job of the manager into five basic tasks. The manager, he wrote, does the following:

1. **Sets objectives.** The manager sets goals for the group and decides what work needs to be done to meet those goals.

2. **Organizes.** The manager divides the work into manageable activities and selects people to accomplish the tasks.

3. **Motivates and communicates.** The manager creates a team out of his or her people through decisions on pay, placement, and promotion and through his or her communications with the team. Drucker referred to this as the "integrating" function of the manager.

4. **Measures.** The manager establishes appropriate targets and yardsticks and analyzes, appraises, and interprets performance.

5. **Develops people.** With the rise of the knowledge worker, this task has taken on added importance. In a so-called knowledge economy, people are the company's most important asset, and it is up to the manager to develop that asset. When a manager learns, understands, and puts into action those five basic tasks, measuring how well the manager is performing his or her job becomes fairly easy.

Question to self: How am I performing in these five tasks?

Now take the case of an executive assistant - that all-important position in a company that determines whether a senior executive can easily move through her or his myriad of daily demands.

WHAT DEFINES AN EFFECTIVE EXECUTIVE ASSISTANT?

The effective executive assistant (EEA) builds value for a business by supporting the executive in such a manner that he or she is able to more effectively perform his or her job.

Let's break this down further and look at the precise skills of an EEA.

THE CORE COMPETENCIES

The EEA provides nearly invisible support for the executive, acting with little supervision and anticipating needs while managing the day-to-day workflow and prioritizing various projects.

There are nine core competencies of an EEA.

1. **Adaptability**
   - demonstrates flexibility in the face of change
   - projects a positive, helpful demeanor regardless of changes in working conditions
   - shows the ability to manage multiple conflicting priorities without loss of composure

2. **Organization**
   - determines the appropriate allocation of time (time management)
   - effectively manages the work space, including keeping a clean and organized office, appropriately handling all paper work, and maintaining control over the physical environment (space management)
   - balances conflicting priorities in order to manage work flow, ensure the completion of essential projects, and meet critical deadlines (task management)

3. **Proactive Anticipation of Needs**
   - demonstrates the ability to foresee problems and prevent them by taking action

- utilizes analytical skills and a broad understanding of the business to effectively interpret needs

4. **Communication Skills**
   - understands that the most important aspect of communication is the act of listening and actively works to improve those skills
   - speaks with confidence, uses clear, concise sentences, and is easily understood
   - produces well-thought-out, professional correspondence free of grammatical and spelling errors
   - uses high-quality, professional oral and written skills (as described above) to project a positive image of the business in telephone and electronic interactions

5. **Client Service**
   - interacts professionally with clients and associates at all times
   - promptly responds to requests with accuracy and a courteous demeanor

6. **Broad Understanding of Business Concepts**
   - demonstrates an awareness of fundamental business principles as well as an understanding of the overall industry in which the business operates

7. **Willingness to Be a Team Player**
   - works as a competent member of the team, willingly providing backup support for coworkers when appropriate and actively supporting group goals

8. **Technical Skills**
   - displays proficiency using standard office equipment, such as a computer, fax, photocopier, scanner, and the like
   - demonstrates advanced proficiency by quickly adapting to new technology and easily acquiring new technical skills

9. **Judgment**
   - exhibits sound judgment and the ability to make reasonable decision in the absence of direction
   - swiftly refers problems to the appropriate person(s) when necessary
   - works effectively without constant and direct supervision or guidance

With all of the above tasks and goals clearly outlined and communicated to an executive assistant, the leader or manager can assess how competent and motivated the EA is in each area.

Having clearly defined tasks and goals and demonstrating what a good job looks like sets the scene for the next stage in the leader/follower dialogue.

These clearly defined elements are the fodder for two-way communication between a leader and his or her followers. They also are necessary for implementing the sixth step in the $P = MC^3$ process.

Effective descriptions of specific tasks or goals have three parts:

(1) illustration of what a job done well looks like, or *performance*;

(2) the conditions under which the employee is to perform; and

(3) the criteria for judging the success of the completed task.

Example:

Given a cash register, a credit card authorization system, twelve grocery orders, and twelve different credit cards (conditions), clerks will be able to accurately (criteria) *submit, within one hour of ending a shift, credit card vouchers for approval* (performance).

If you want people to do anything with what you teach them, you must include these three elements - conditions, criteria, and performance.

THE RULES FOR ARTICULATING SPECIFIC TASK AND GOALS

The basic principle of the rules below is this:

If you, as a leader or manager, cannot explain it, followers will not be able to do it well.

1. When judging the performance of a task, ask yourself the following three questions: What is the main intent? What will the employee be doing that demonstrates success? How good is good enough in this instance?

2. Make sure that the intent of the task is known by the follower. Problems occur if the reason to do it is not clear.

3. Individual tasks or goals must be differentiated from team tasks or goals.

4. Each team member must know how what he or she does contributes to team success.

5. Always convey what a good job looks like, including a time frame. Followers will be confused if your expectations are too vague.

To ensure clear understanding, ask followers to jot down what they understand the description of the task to be, including performance, conditions, and criteria.

This process may seem to be a bit detailed, but when you consider the costs of mistakes and misunderstandings, the ROI is worth it.

In the space below, please describe one of your direct report's specific tasks or goals that you would like him or her to improve on.

_____

_____

_____

We will come back to this later.

Step 1: — Get Clear on *"The Deal"*

Step 2: — Align Your People with the Company's Values, Vision, and Mission.

Step 3: - Define the Specific Task or Goal

STEP 4: DIAGNOSE, AND AGREE ON, THE SPECIFIC TASK/GOAL COMPETENCE AND MOTIVATION (CM) LEVELS

Determine

    Inspire

        Ask

            Ground

                Negotiate

                    Organize

                        See

                            Evaluate

Why diagnose? To zero in on what leader style the person or team needs in order to perform at a high level.

Competence and motivation are two interrelated but distinctly different aspects of a person's job performance. It is important to not confuse the two.

To diagnose competence and motivation, work with observed behaviours. Use the video test to identify observed behaviours. Do not make an assessment of the person's attitudes, hopes, and other vagaries.

The typical manager might make the following statements:

You must do better!
You have to change your attitude!
You have to give better customer service.
You have to try harder!

Those admonitions do not help a person improve his or her performance.

In *Leadership for Einsteins*, we work with behaviours because they can easily be observed, recorded (in one's mind or electronically), described, slowed down, and analyzed.

THE VIDEO TEST

You can use *"The Video Test"* to improve, duplicate, repeat, or eliminate behaviours.

Effective leaders and managers spell out very specific behaviours that will clearly demonstrate when a job is done well - or not.

For example: *"A job well done is when you can answer the phone in a courteous manner while listening to the clients concerns (even if they may be angry upset) and addressing them in a helpful, cheerful way."*

Being able and willing to articulate behaviours is the most effective, time-efficient way to achieve measureable, consistent improvement in performance. When leaders and managers help workers to improve their results based on feedback on their behaviours, employees' attitudes shift dramatically towards the positive.

"The Video Test" is a tool to tell the difference between what people are saying or what they think they are doing from what they are actually saying or doing.

When I was being trained to facilitate groups, I was often asked to conduct an experience with a group under the watchful eyes of my mentors. After each session, we would meet to debrief, with honest feedback and feedforward, about what I had done, how I had done it, why I had done it, and how I could improve.

They would say, *"We saw you being aggressive and interrupting people."*

I would respond defensively with, *"I didn't do that!"*

The sessions were always videotaped.

"Play the tape!" they would say.

And there I was, exposed and embarrassed about what I had done. It was a most useful, though difficult, learning experience.

Managers are often guilty of judging people on their attitudes rather than their behaviours, relying on what people say they are going to do and then being disappointed when "the say" and "the do" don't match, and not actually seeing what their direct report is doing - or not doing - because of some prejudgment.

Here's how *"The Video Test"* works. Imagine you are recording the activities of people, and then describing only what you see and hear. When you use *"The Video Test,"* you look, watch, and describe the behaviours of the person:

"I noticed that you were twenty-five minutes late for work today."

"When the customer got angry, you stopped and listened to him. He then calmed right down."

Why do this? Because people's behaviours can be observed, recorded, slowed down, and analyzed so they can be improved, duplicated, or eliminated.

"The Video Test" eliminates a great deal of emotional turbulence when you are giving and receiving feedback. It allows you to step back and consider how you can best connect with an individual using feedback and feedforward. This reduces the emotional charge because people are more open to hearing a behaviour described than a judgment proclaimed.

Pretty simple. Very powerful.

For a detailed description of feedforward, e-mail me at jim@subject2change.ca.

Action step to practice *"The Video Test"*:

For half a day, step back and observe the behaviours of your team members. Do not make comments. Write down some of their behaviours so you can refer back to them.

Question: Do you go on employees' attitudes, or what they say. Or do you mostly rely on their behaviours to improve their performances? How is that working for you?

COMPETENCE

Competence is the ability to carry out a specific task or goal to consistently produce the desired results. It is made up of the following:

- **Technical Skills**
  Technical job skills are the sets of knowledge and capabilities that a person possesses to perform a certain job or task, often referred to as "hard skills" (e.g., an accountant knowing how to read and interpret a balance sheet).

- **Emotional Intelligence (EI) or Interpersonal Skills**
  EI is made up of the following:
  - awareness of one's behaviours and how those behaviours affect others
  - self-management, or being able and willing to direct one's behaviours in order to bring out one's unique talents
  - empathy, or the ability and willingness to understand another's situation, feelings, and motives
  - social skills, including the ability and willingness to "play well with others"
  - assertiveness, which includes speaking up and respectfully asserting one's opinion in a team setting

- **Job Knowledge**
  Employee has developed the skills to do the job in a particular company.

- **Organizational Power and Influence**
  Organizational *power* is having the authority to do things based on one's defined position, such as CEO, CFO, or operations manager. This power is given (and can be taken away) by the organization.

  Organizational *influence* is other people's willingness to follow the person's directives because the person is recognized, respected and valued. This, too, can be taken away at any time.

Competence is diagnosed as follows:

- C_2 (high): The individual has all the technical skills, emotional intelligence, job knowledge, and organizational power and/or influence to do the task/job consistently and well, with little to no supervision.
- C_1 (moderate): The individual has some of the four elements, does well most of the time, and needs some supervision.
- C_0 (low): The individual lacks the skills needed to do the task/job well and needs close supervision to develop the skills.

Competence is task/goal specific.

A line worker who has developed high competence as a line worker might be promoted to production manager.

It is highly likely that in the new role of production manager, he or she will drop into a low competence level because being a manager calls for a different set of skills than those of a line worker.

This is why such a high percentage of people who get promoted do not live up to expectations. The organization fails them by not onboarding and developing them to learn the new set of competencies to do well in their new role.

Practice diagnosing your competence.

First, think about a task that you would diagnose yourself as low competence. (yes we all have one or two of those.) Briefly describe the task in writing. Are you low in technical skills, emotional intelligence, job knowledge and/or organizational power and influence. What help might you need to increase your competence.

Note: You may choose to not put an effort into increasing your competence because you are not motivated to do so. Then your responsibility is to find someone who can do that task for you.

Second, think about a task that you would diagnose yourself as high competence. Briefly describe the task in writing. Are you strong in the four areas? To test the accuracy of your diagnosis, ask your boss whether he or she thinks you perform competently in that task.

MOTIVATION

Motivation is the willingness to persist towards completing a specific task or achieving a goal in spite of challenges or setbacks. It is a combination of several elements, outlined below:

- **Interest**

    Interest can be seen in behaviours that demonstrate that the person or team wants to achieve a specific task or goal.

    For example, if I say I am interested in learning how to read a balance sheet and I get instructions from someone who knows how to do so and I practice doing a few readings while asking for feedback from that person, then I am authentically interested.

    If I say I'm interested in learning how to read a balance sheet, but don't "put my money where my mouth is" then I'm not really interested.

- **Risk Taking and Self-Confidence**

    A worker with self-confidence has the willingness to "go out on a limb"—to try things without knowing the outcome.

    There are two things to keep in mind here. First, you want people to take risks appropriate to their level of skills and experience. Second, self-confidence is built by taking risks and learning how to do things better. First comes risk; then comes confidence.

- **Alignment with Company Goals**

    When someone signs up to work at a company, he or she agrees to do his or her best to achieve the company's stated goals because that's what the deal is all about. The company's responsibility is to clearly outline the goals.

- **Willingness to Assume Responsibility**
  The willingness to carry forward an assigned task to a successful conclusion.

- **Willingness to be Accountable**
  Accountability in the context of teamwork refers specifically to the willingness of all team members to embrace responsibility, the relentless pursuit of team results, and the willingness to call out peers on behaviours that hurt the team.

Motivation is diagnosed as follows:

- M_2 (high): The individual exceeds expectations on a specific goal/task shown in interest, risk taking, alignment with company goals, individual responsibility, or team accountability.
- M_1 (moderate): The individual meets expectations on a specific goal/task in each of the four elements.
- M_0 (low): The individual does not meet expectations on a specific goal/task in the four elements.

Each of the four task- or goal-specific competence and motivation levels calls for a different leader style. You learn how to do that in step 5 below.

TIME TO START PLAYING

Please go back to p. 47 and review your description of the task or goal you want a person to improve.

Now diagnose the task-specific competence level.

Is it, in your opinion, C_2,(high) C_1 (moderate) or C_0 (low)?

Quick reminder: Competence is made up of task-specific technical skills, emotional intelligence (EI) or interpersonal skills, job knowledge, and organizational power and influence.

Now diagnose the task-specific motivational level.

Is it, in your opinion, M_2,(high) M_1, (moderate) or M_0 (low)?

Quick reminder: Motivation is a combination of interest, risk taking and self-confidence, alignment with company goals, willingness to assume responsibility as an individual, and willingness to be accountable to a team.

EMOTIONAL INTELLIGENCE IS THE OXYGEN OF LEADERSHIP

Emotional intelligence is the ability to monitor one's own and others' feelings and emotions, to discriminate among them, and to use this information to guide one's thinking and actions.[18]

Here are some descriptions of the three levels of emotional intelligence:

Low EI

"My manager is terrible at expressing his emotions."

Moderate EI

"My manager is fairly level-headed most of the time but if he gets stressed he 'blows his top' and blames people for any screw-ups."

High EI

"My teammate takes into consideration how everyone else on the team is feeling."

"The CEO is brilliant at dealing with her employees' emotions—a real motivator!"

"My teammates take time to listen before responding to people's ideas."

". . . my research, along with other recent studies, clearly shows that emotional intelligence is the sine qua non of leadership. Without it, a person can have the best training in the world, an incisive, analytical mind, and an endless supply of smart ideas, but s/he still won't make a great leader."
Daniel Goleman, *Harvard Business Review*[19]

A basic operating assumption in *Leadership for Einsteins* is that a leader, manager, supervisor, or follower is effective to the degree that he or she has developed his or her emotional intelligence.

The link between emotional intelligence and leadership was shown at PepsiCo.

Executives selected for EI competencies outperformed their colleagues, delivering the following:

- 10 percent increase in productivity
- 87 percent decrease in executive turnover ($4 million savings)
- $4 million added economic value
- About 1,000 percent ROI.[20]

Step 1: – Get Clear on *"The Deal"*

Step 2: – Align Your People with the Company's Values, Vision, and Mission.

Step 3: - Define The Specific Task Or Goal

Step 4: Diagnose and Agree On the Competence and Motivation Levels

STEP 5: CHOOSE THE LEADER STYLE THAT BEST FITS THE TASK/ GOAL SPECIFIC COMPETENCE AND MOTIVATION LEVELS

Leadership is about

LONG-TERM VISION
  EXCELLENCE
    ACTION
      DIAGNOSING
        ENCOURAGING
          RESPONSIBILITY
            SELF-AWARENESS
              HUMILITY
                INFLUENCING
                  PERSEVERING

- To engage, align, and work *with* people

WHAT I TEACH IS WHAT I GET

People do not do what they are supposed to do because the leader or manager has not taught them the following:

- what tasks or goals need to be done
- how to do the tasks or goals well
- why the tasks or goals need to be done
- by when those tasks or goals are to be completed
- how to engage in a two-way conversation with the leader or manager to make sure the process stays on track

Two basic leadership behaviours are (1) *showing* and (2) *encouraging*.

Showing people how to do a task includes giving lots of specific feedback to increase their competencies and build a sense of achievement so they can perform at an increasingly higher level.

Showing outlines who will do what and by when, why it must be done, and how it will get done. It is about teaching, instructing, demonstrating, and onboarding.

Encouraging individuals and teams to improve performance means increasing motivation in order to leverage their competencies into higher value to the company while increasing their personal satisfaction.

You are *encouraging* when you listen to and acknowledge employees' difficulties, confusions, concerns or input. You are encouraging when you recognize followers' capabilities and efforts.

You are *encouraging* when you show a workplace appropriate interest in their personal life.

Use Showing When....	Use Encouraging When....
• Person or Team = Task Specific Low Competence. • The Process is non-negotiable. • I need to make sure, up-front, that people understand what to do, when to do it, and how to do it. • The individual/team is just starting out. • Buy-in isn't crucial (i.e. No decision being made), we're just at the exploratory stage. • Time is very limited. • It's an emergency and a decision must be made quickly. • The individual/team is new and requires specifics around mandate, expectations, etc. • The task requires the expertise I posses and many people don't have it so I need to show them how to do it.	• *Person or Team = Task Specific Moderate to High Competence.* • *I need to build buy-in amongst members.* • *The Individual/team is per forming competently, needs some confidence boosting.* • *People are able and willing to be part of the process, and I want them to "get" that they are able.* • *It's vital the person/group feels empowered.* • *I have time to engage in a two-way discussion.* • *I am not the subject matter expert and this expertise is required to achieve the goal or complete the task.* • *I'm dealing with decreasing performance: probe and listen to find out - why?*

THE FOUR LEADER STYLES

To get a free colour pdf of the four leader styles, go to http://www.subject2change.ca/colour.

L_1: SHOWING (BEST WITH TASK-SPECIFIC C_0M_1 AND C_1M_0)

The L_1 leader style involves ***lots of showing behaviours*** and *some encouraging behaviours*. The leader is the decision maker. He or she provides specific instructions and supervises followers closely to develop competencies.

Showing behaviours allow a leader or manager to get clear on *"The Deal;"* engage and align workers with the company's values, vision, and mission; make sure the right people are on the bus and doing the right things; and teach the what, why, how, and by when.

This style is seen as authoritarian by individuals with higher levels of task-specific competence and motivation. Such individuals may be thinking, *"Get out of my face! Do you think I'm an idiot?"*

*"When recruiting baristas, Starbucks looks for people with outgoing personalities and strong social skills (two markers of emotional intelligence). To convey these attributes and prompt customer-savvy individuals to self-select into the firm, Starbucks tells all prospective hires about its mandatory in-store immersion process (**showing** leadership style). Every new Starbucks employee - even at the corporate level - goes through a 24-hour paid training module called First Impressions. The standardized curriculum focuses on learning about coffee and creating*

*a positive customer experience. In-store training follows - employees are **shown** how to make beverages, talk to customers, and learn the business on the floor (**showing**). Employees at all levels say this hands-on being **shown the what, why, how & by when** experience is essential preparation for any role within the company.*

They swap stories about candidates who ditched the process early on (C_0M_0s - will not follow, cannot be led), because they didn't want to work at Starbucks.

The satisfied people (C_0M_1s - enthusiastic learners) who stuck with it, tell these tales with great pride."

L_2: FOCUSING (BEST WITH TASK-SPECIFIC C_2M_0, C_0M_2 AND C_1M_1)

The second leader style, L_2, involves **lots of showing** and **lots of encouraging** behaviours. The leader or manager with this style explains decisions and provides followers with opportunities for clarification, asks questions to assess competence and motivation levels, and instructs or informs so that workers can increase task performance.

In short, the leader makes decisions while listening to and considering input from followers. Performance is measured by the accuracy, thoroughness, effectiveness, and efficiency of task performance.

Two effective ways to increase performance using a ***focusing*** style are (1) selectively assigning tasks according to the person's or team's present level of competency and motivation and (2) systematically developing and showing appreciation for the person's or team's value to the organization by increasing their competencies and motivation. Both of these methods require regular check-ins.

When this style is used with workers who have higher levels of task-specific competence, they tend to see it as interfering. They may think, *"Why are you asking me this? Why are you telling me this - I already know how to do it!"*

Focusing is a key onboarding process style. Use this style big-time in the ninety-day probationary period to find out whether you've made a good hire or not.

L_3: FACILITATING (BEST WITH TASK-SPECIFIC C_1M_2, C_2M_1)

A *facilitating* leader style involves **lots of encouraging** behaviours and *some showing* behaviours. This type of leader or manager shares ideas with followers and facilitates decision making while drawing out each person's developing competencies.

- Leader shares decision-making with followers.
- Equally task-specific competent coworkers collaborate to explore issues and solve problems with two-way conversations.
- All engage in active listening.

Even as the CM level continues to increase, most developing employees go through a self-doubt phase in which they question whether they can perform the task on their own (C_2), even though they may have done it well in the past.

At those times, they need a *facilitating* style to help them get over the hump and build internal motivation. They need to be listened to in order to explore their doubts and recognize their competencies. They need encouragement to draw out of them what they know and how they can apply it.

They do not need a lot of showing since they have demonstrated increasing competence for doing the task based on the video test.

Eight *Facilitating* Questions

1. What options do you see at this point?
2. What steps have you been considering that we can take now?
3. What options haven't we tried yet?
4. Have we missed any important aspects of this issue?
5. How soon can you get started?
6. Do you need anything to get started?
7. What do you think we could do to help us accurately track this project?
8. What's one thing you could do to make a difference in this task?

The facilitating style, when used with individuals who have not yet developed task-specific competencies or motivation is irrelevant and demotivating. People who have lower-level task-specific competence or motivation cannot answer the above eight questions. *"Why are you asking?"* they wonder. *"I don't know how to do it yet!"*

L_4: DELEGATING (BEST WITH C_2M_2)

The ***delegating*** leader style uses *some encouraging* behaviours and *some showing* behaviours. The leader turns over responsibility for decisions and implementation to followers because they have demonstrated a high level of competence and motivation for the task or goal.

Effective ***delegating*** means allocating decision-making authority, task responsibility, or both to others to maximize the individual's, team's, and organization's effectiveness. Competent **delegation** saves time, develops people, grooms successors, and motivates.

Incompetent delegation, or abdicating, results in frustration, demotivation, and confusion. Delegating incompetently also leads to so-called seagull behaviours of managers.

A seagull behaviour is telling the low-competence employees what to do and leaving them alone to do it, only to come back later to berate them for screwing up. This style, when used with workers whose task-specific competencies or motivations are not yet developed, is a form of abdicating. A worker's typical response is, *"I have no clue about what I'm supposed to do next!"*

LEADER STYLES IN A BOX

L2 - FOCUSING
    Lots of Encouragement
    Lots of Showing
• Use with C_1M_2, C_1M_1, C_2M_0
 	
Leader, Co-worker...
• Decides with input from direct reports
• Listens, then informs, corrects or praises
• Praises followers for making suggestions
• Rewards for progress or,
• Lays out consequences for failure to preform (regression)
	L2 - FACILITATING
	    Lots of Encouragement
	    Some Showing
	• Best with C_1M_2, C_2M_1
	
	Leader, Colleague...
	• Encourages followers' decision making
	• Listens actively to increase Motivation to leverage competence
	• Praises direct reports for asking for input
	• Provides showing input only when necessary

L1 - SHOWING
    Lots of Showing
    Some encouragement
• Most helpful with **CoM_1, C_1M_0**
 	
Leader, Coach, Co-worker...
• Decides without much input
• Shows what, when, why, and how
• Praises followers for trying and complying
• Instructs to increase Competence
• Checks in, tracks progress
	L4 - DELEGATING
	    Some Encouragement
	    Some Showing
	• Use with C_2M_2
	
	Leader, Mentor...
	• Lets direct reports decide
	• Maintains limited task communication
	• Praises followers for assuming responsibility
	• Asks to be kept informed

LET'S LEARN, PRACTICE, AND PLAY TO DIAGNOSE, AND MATCH LEADERSHIP STYLES

So people will be doing what they're supposed to be doing - and doing it well.

CASE 1

In order to strengthen my department, I have recently brought in some new talent. As these new people spend time with me on interesting assignments, Jack, who has been here for years, is becoming more demotivated. His performance is dropping. He still has good skills but is not using them.

Your first step is to diagnose his task-specific competence and motivation levels. The task in question is becoming an effective team member. I would diagnose him as $C_1 M_1$: some competence, moderate motivation. His behaviours demonstrate that he does not know how to include himself in the new team. As a result, his motivation is dropping.

Your options, based on the different leader styles, are as follows:

A. Ask him about his assignments and give him support on them.
Style: facilitating/irrelevant.
This style might work but is risky because Jack is demotivated. He needs some more direction to lift him out of his funk.

B. Wait for him to approach me first.
Style: delegating/abdicating.
This style would not be helpful to getting Jack back on track. It is too wishy-washy. He needs a gentle but definite intervention.

C. Ask him about his assignments. Then lay out clear expectations for each.

Style: focusing
Focusing is the high-probability style, the style that is likely to be helpful to Jack so that he can become an effective team member.

D. Lay out clear expectations for each of his assignments. Be explicit about what he should be doing.
Style: showing/dictatorial
This style is too directive and not encouraging enough, since he has a history of doing well.

QUICK REMINDER

Competence is determined by task- or goal-specific technical skills, emotional intelligence, job knowledge, and organizational power and influence.

Motivation is task- or goal-specific interest, willingness to take risks, alignment with organizational goals, and possession of individual responsibility or team accountability

CASE 2

Sarah heads up an important part of my department. Her get-it-done behaviours offset her relative lack of experience and occasional errors in judgment. Her unit is very cohesive and usually rises to a good challenge. A major project in Sarah's area has been assigned to my department.

Sarah's task is working on a major project. Her task-specific competence and motivation level is C_0M_2 low competence and high motivation. She does not have the competence to do the task without direction because of her lack of experience, as evidenced by her occasional errors. However, she is highly motivated to take on the project.

Below are the options for this case, based on the different leader styles:

A. Tell Sarah about the project's importance. Outline a detailed plan for its completion.
Style: showing/dictatorial
This style is too directive and does not take advantage of Sarah's high level of motivation.

B. Invite Sarah to offer input as I develop the project plan.
Style: focusing
Sarah does not have a high enough level of competence to contribute much just yet, but I do want to build on her enthusiasm by engaging her in the planning conversation. By engaging her, I can give her more helpful direction.

C. Ask Sarah to develop the project plan and discuss it with me before going ahead with it.
Style: facilitating/irrelevant
Sarah does not have a high enough level of task-specific competency to take on the planning of the project. She is likely to fail or become confused and demotivated with this style.

D. Ask Sarah to handle the project and to keep me informed of the group's progress.
Style: delegating/abdicating
This style would be abdicating, not delegating, which would probably result in the project failing for Sarah and me.

You can always tell whether your leadership style is effective. If you're close to matching your leadership style with people's task-specific competence and motivation levels, they will be doing what they are supposed to be doing. If, on the other hand, your leadership style does not match the task-specific competence and motivation levels, you're way off the mark, and people will not be doing what they are supposed to be doing.

CASE 3

George has only been with my department for a few months working in an area that is new to him. He is starting to learn the job requirements. He is still reluctant to take on much responsibility. My boss has just requested—with a tight deadline—a report George is working on.

George's task is to deliver a "good" report on a tight deadline. I would diagnose his level as C_0M_1. His task-specific competence is low, and his motivation is moderate.

The following are the options for this case based on the different leader styles:

A. Ask him what he has done so far. Help him to develop his own plan for finishing it.
   Style: facilitating/irrelevant
   This style is risky. George is just learning the job requirements, and my boss wants that report stat!

B. Let him know the boss wants to see the report ASAP.
   Style: delegating/abdicating
   This style is a recipe for disaster for George. I will bear the wrath of my boss if the report is done badly or submitted late. George will feel the seagull droppings.

C. Go over the report in detail and show him exactly how it should be done.
   Ask him to check in with his progress on a daily basis.
   Style: showing
   Given the tight deadline, George's low task-specific competence level, and his reluctance to take on much responsibility, this style has a good chance of being very helpful to George getting the report done on time.
   Daily check-ins will be seen as supportive by George.

D. Ask him what he has done so far, and then show him how to finish the report properly.
Style: focusing/interfering
This style is too loose given the parameters, particularly the tight deadline.

CASE 4

I inherited Steve when I took over the department. His technical skills are adequate, but his lack of political savvy and interpersonal skills limits him. He is a hard worker but lacks the confidence to handle some aspects of his job.

Steve has moderate competence and moderate motivation to do the identified task – develop his technical skills as well as his political savvy and emotional intelligence. I would give him a C_1M_1 diagnosis.
Here are the options for Steve based on the different leader styles:

A. Stay out of his way so that he can develop at his own pace.
Style: delegating/abdicating
This style would not develop Steve's technical skills; I would fail in my duties as a manager to develop Steve.

B. Give him clear assignments. Supervise him carefully.
Style: showing/dictatorial
I think if I used this style, Steve would judge me as being a bit dictatorial and would start resisting my efforts. In turn, I would become frustrated with him.

C. Talk with him about his strengths and weaknesses, and then structure his assignments to help him develop.
Style: focusing
In this two-way conversation, Steve could outline what he needs. I could, based on what Steve is saying, show him how to increase his technical skills. By listening to Steve for understanding, I

would demonstrate that I want to encourage him, which would bring up his motivation level.

D. Talk with him about his strengths and weaknesses and then work with him to make his own plan for improvement.
Style: facilitating/irrelevant
I think he is not quite ready to make his own plan, but he is likely to be ready fairly quickly by doing option C. I would monitor his progress and shift to this style as he shows progress.

Step 1: – Get Clear on *"The deal"*

Step 2: – Align Your People with the Company's Values, Vision, and Mission.

Step 3: - Define the Specific Task or Goal

Step 4: - Diagnose, and Agree On, the Specific Task/Goal Competence and Motivation (CM) Levels – use *"The Video Test"*

Step 5: Choose The Leader Style That Best Fits the Task-/Goal Specific Competence and Motivation Levels

STEP 6: NEGOTIATING FOR PERFORMANCE TO ENGAGE AND ALIGN PEOPLE

Bad managers are the number-one reason employees quit or, worse yet, quit and stay. They are also responsible when people are not doing what they are supposed to be doing.

We've all experienced a bad manager at some point. Today, 70 percent of North American employees feel indifferent or disengaged at work, costing the US economy nearly $500 billion every year in lost productivity, substandard performance, and employee turnover.

Good managers engage with their employees by having two-way conversations with them. If you want to be a good manager, you must learn how to negotiate for performance.

The big goal of ***negotiating for performance*** is to align employees to the company's values, vision, and mission by reinforcing behaviours that lead to high performance. To put it another way, ***negotiating for performance*** is intended to get people to buy into doing what they are supposed to be doing.

Negotiating solidifies employees' emotional connection with your company, making them more engaged. Two-way conversations are the key ingredient that drives remarkable business success every single day.

When leaders, managers, and supervisors negotiate using two-way conversations, followers feel recognized.

Engaged, aligned, and recognized employees will work harder to satisfy customers and in turn create greater shareholder value. Employee engagement and customer loyalty are inextricably linked. Employees that have been given the training and tools to delight the customer and deliver exemplary service have an attitude of being customer centric, and this translates into higher revenue growth and profitability.

When you reinforce desired behaviours and work to eliminate undesirable behaviours in the *negotiation* process, a culture of continuous improvement is established. Engagement and alignment are the invaluable results of taking a *negotiating* approach to performance. *Negotiating* makes it possible to better leverage your best resources - your people.

Another outcome of taking a *negotiating* approach is that all employees understand the big picture. According to Stephen Covey's research in *The 8th Habit*, only 37 percent of employees have a clear understanding of what their organization is trying to achieve and why. Employees need to understand how they directly impact your business success in order for their work to seem valuable to them.

Alignment and engagement are dependent on leaders and managers. They must communicate the company's objectives and core company values. *Negotiating* with employees to live the core values every day helps to connect employees with the bigger picture and purpose and reinforces the right behaviours for your company.

Effectively *negotiating* via two-way conversations ensures that employees understand what behaviours are being measured and why. Furthermore, companies that develop leaders who are highly effective *negotiators* have a 47 percent higher total shareholder return.[21]

The three whys of *negotiating for performance* are as follows:

1. **To show appreciation**. Make sure your employees know they're important to you. This helps build commitment. Amazingly, 63 percent of organizations don't even tell their highest-performing people that they are appreciated.

2. **To give people a challenge**. Give followers highly visible and challenging tasks. Employees that are most highly engaged are those who get challenging tasks and unconditional support.

3. **To elicit commitment**. In return for your company's investment in them, consider asking your high-performing people and employees who are showing significant improvement to commit to the company for a set period of time. And tell them that you are asking for their commitment because you value them. You must then back up that request with numbers one and two above.

Leadership for Einsteins negotiating principles are as follows:

- "Good" performance cannot be compelled, commanded, or coerced.
- Performance is a voluntary, participative, negotiated sport.
- High performance is developed out of a negotiated partnership, not "because I said so!"
- Performance is a negotiation that arises out of the previous five steps.
  It's about zeroing in on what the person or team members need to understand the task in sufficient detail so they will know what it takes, what help they need, and when it has been achieved at a high level.
- Performance is a process for creating volunteers while eliminating the volun_tolds_.

To get a template for negotiating for performance, go to www.subject2change.ca/LfE/negotiate

Since you have read this far and you have filled out the negotiating template I am offering you a free executive leadership coaching session (I usually charge $675 for coaching) to answer any questions you may have.

You can email me jim@subject2change.ca to arrange a time.

So that's the road map - the big picture - the six steps to working with people so they are doing what they are supposed to be doing.

Step 1: Get Clear on *"The Deal"*

Step 2: Align Your People with the Company's Values, Vision, and Mission

Step 3: Define the Specific Task or Goal

Step 4: Diagnose and Agree On the Competence and Motivation Levels — Use *"The Video Test"*

Step 5: Choose the Leadership Style That Best Fits the Task-Specific Competence and Motivation Levels

Step 6: Negotiate for Performance to Engage and Align People

Are you willing?

Check out my ebook *Account-Ability – The Science of Human Performance* on Kindle

I would very much appreciate it if you would do an honest review of this book and put it on Kindle reviews. Thank you.

NOTES

(Endnotes)

1 Stephen R. Covey, *The 8th Habit: From Effectiveness to Greatness* (New York: Free Press, 2004) 289.

2 Source: survey of 2450 employers from CareerBuilder.com

3 http://www.watsonwyatt.com/search/publications.asp?Component=wwme&ArticleID=11551

4 http://humanresources.about.com/cs/strategicplanning1/a/strategic-plan.html

5 http://bit.ly/1pU5cCK

6 http://abt.cm/1jpqAdj

7 http://bit.ly/TnL2Et

8 Active Leadership at the Gap, Old Navy, 2005.

9 Cost of turnover is estimated to start at about $7500 and run up to $25,000. Depending on the position. You have to account for lost productivity from exited employee, search costs, interviewing costs, training costs and administrative costs until the new hire is competent.

10 http://www.accenture.com/Global/Services/By_Subject/Workforce_Performance/R_and_I/TransformingAchieveHP.html

11 http://www.accenture.com/Global/Research_and_Insights/Outlook/By_Subject/Human_Resource_Mgmt/ReturnLearningPart3.html

12 The 2000 Ig Nobel Prize Winners. Improbable Research.

13 Justin Kruger and David Dunning, "Unskilled and Unaware of It: How Difficulties in
Recognizing One's Own Incompetence Lead to Inflated Self-Assessments," *Journal of*

Personality and Social Psychology 77, no. 6 (1999): 1121–34.

14 http://www.vancitycareers.com/feelExperience/partnership.html

15 Presence: Human Purpose and the Field of the Future Peter Senge, C. Otto Scharmer, Joseph Jaworski, Betty Sue Flowers, SoL, March 2004.

16 http://www.watsonwyatt.com/canada-english/

17 http://www.druckerinstitute.com/peter-druckers-life-and-legacy/ The End of Economic Man.

18 Peter Salovey. Yale University. John D. *Mayer*. University of New Hampshire. Emotional intelligence. 1990: 189.

19 http://hbr.org/2004/01/what-makes-a-leader/ar/1

20 http://www.talentmgt.com/articles/emotional_intelligence_tied_to_leadership_success and Berg Consulting: A Business Case for Emotional Intelligent Leaders – Hand Out.

21 (Capitalizing on Effective Communication: How Courage, Innovation and Discipline Drive Business Results in Challenging Times, Towers Watson. 2010. Web. Feb. 2014)

Made in the USA
Charleston, SC
04 February 2015